Prairie
ABCs

Jocey Asnong

RMB

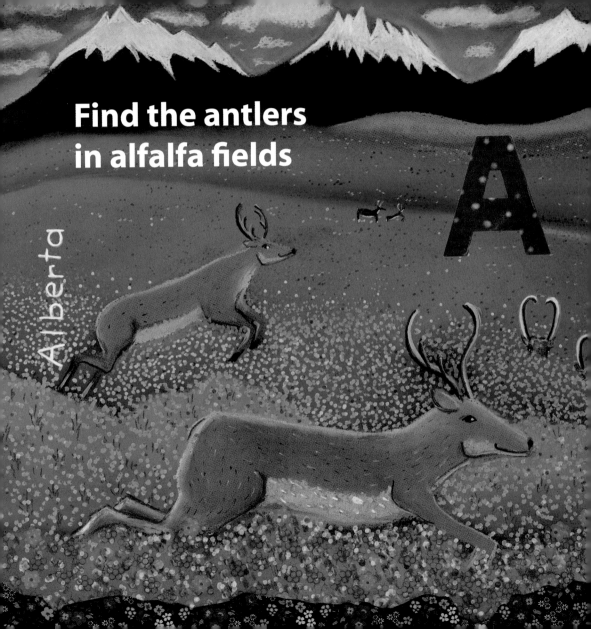

Find the antlers
in alfalfa fields

Bison roam
between birch trees

Bagwa Lake, Saskatchewan

B

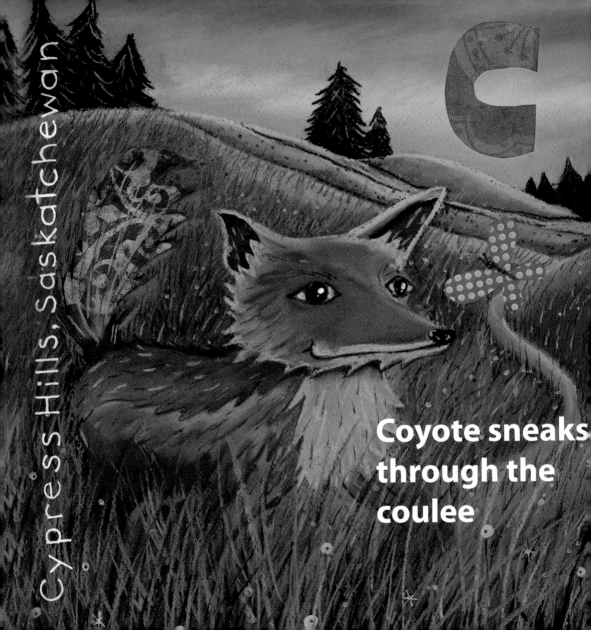

Cypress Hills, Saskatchewan

Coyote sneaks through the coulee

Pretend we hear the dinosaurs roar

Drumheller, Alberta

Esther, Alberta

Elevators rise into prairie skies

Our farm is ready for fall

Foxwarren.Manitoba

Horse gallops through high grasses

Gimli, Manitoba

We invite mice
to skate on our ice

Imperial, Saskatchewan

Kittens jump for our kite's tail

Kindersley, Saskatchewan

J K

Longhorns wade in the lake

Lloydminster, Alberta/Saskatchewan

Moose might kiss
in the morning mist

Manitoba

N

Now it's time
for a nap

Neepawa, Manitoba

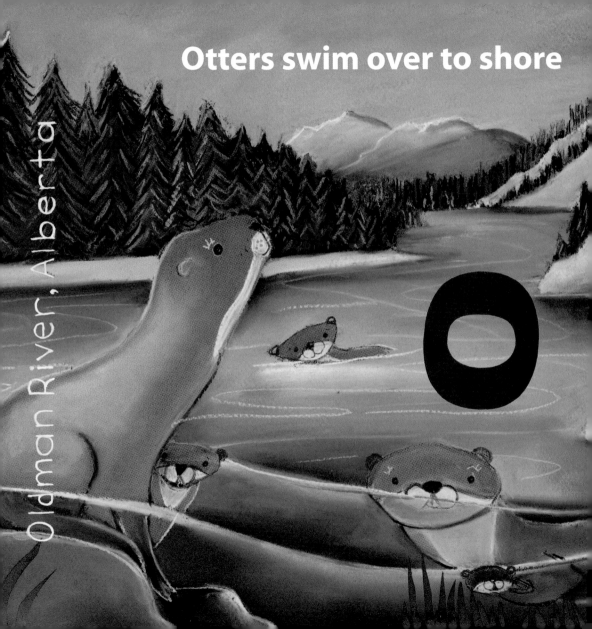

Otters swim over to shore

Oldman River, Alberta

**Put on our parkas
for prairie winds**

Portage la Prairie, Manitoba

Riding Mountain National Park, Manitoba

QR

Look quickly, it's a rainbow!

S Squirrels snack on summer berries

Saskatchewan

Three Hills, Alberta

Take our tractor through the fields

We harvest wheat
before winter comes

Winter, Manitoba

Lynx looks both ways
at railway x-ing

Xena, Saskatchewan

Young bee drinks
from yellow flowers

Youngstown, Alberta

Zealandia, Saskatchewan.

For information on purchasing bulk quantities of this book, or to obtain media excerpts or invite the author to speak at an event, please visit rmbooks.com and select the "Contact" tab.

RMB | Rocky Mountain Books Ltd.
rmbooks.com
@rmbooks
facebook.com/rmbooks

Cataloguing data available from Library and Archives Canada
ISBN 9781771604970 (board book)
ISBN 9781771604987 (softcover)
ISBN 9781771604994 (electronic)

Printed and bound in China

We would like to also take this opportunity to acknowledge the traditional territories upon which we live and work. In Calgary, Alberta, we acknowledge the Niitsítapi (Blackfoot) and the people of the Treaty 7 region in Southern Alberta, which includes the Siksika, the Piikuni, the Kainai, the Tsuut'ina, and the Stoney Nakoda First Nations, including Chiniki, Bearpaw, and Wesley First Nations. The City of Calgary is also home to Métis Nation of Alberta, Region III. In Victoria, British Columbia, we acknowledge the traditional territories of the Lkwungen (Esquimalt and Songhees), Malahat, Pacheedaht, Scia'new, T'Sou-ke, and W̱SÁNEĆ (Pauquachin, Tsartlip, Tsawout, Tseycum) peoples.

We acknowledge the financial support of the Government of Canada through the Canada Book Fund and the Canada Council for the Arts, and of the province of British Columbia through the British Columbia Arts Council and the Book Publishing Tax Credit.

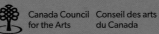
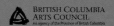